Bible Of Comfort:
Biblical Wisdom for Healing During Troubled Times

University Scholastic Press

In times of turmoil and tribulation, the Bible remains a timeless source of solace, guidance, and wisdom. *Bible Of Comfort: Biblical Wisdom for Healing During Troubled Times,* curated by the esteemed international publisher, University Scholastic Press, offers a poignant compilation of scripture passages, meticulously organized to address the profound and often tumultuous emotions that accompany life's most challenging moments.

Within these pages lies a comprehensive anthology of divine counsel, focusing on ten profound emotions that touch the core of human existence. From the fiery grasp of anger to the weighty burdens of grief, loneliness, and fear, this illuminating volume meticulously navigates the scriptures to uncover divine insights that offer hope, healing, and resilience.

Each section meticulously assembles verses and teachings from the Bible that speak directly to the heart of the emotion at hand. For those grappling with anxiety, passages of reassurance and strength are carefully selected. To those wrestling with despair or poverty, the verses offer empathy and a beacon of hope. The anguish of regret and shame finds solace in the verses that preach redemption, forgiveness, and a path towards healing.

This masterfully curated book transcends religious boundaries, offering a universal balm for the human soul. It serves as a companion for anyone seeking solace, encouragement, and a deeper spiritual understanding during life's most challenging moments. Whether you turn to it for personal reflection, pastoral guidance, or communal support, *Bible Of Comfort* stands as an indispensable resource, offering timeless insights that resonate across generations and cultures.

Bible Of Comfort isn't merely a book; it's a sanctuary—a refuge to turn to when the storms of life rage and the weight of emotions becomes unbearable. It stands as a testament to the enduring power of faith, compassion, and the unwavering promise of healing found within the sacred verses of the Bible. Universally resonant and profoundly comforting, this volume stands as a beacon of hope, inviting readers to discover the boundless strength and solace found within its pages.

Table Of Contents

Introduction

The Bible serves as a source of guidance, comfort, and wisdom for navigating through various negative emotions. It offers solace and support when we're experiencing distress, sadness, anxiety, anger, and other challenging emotions, providing valuable insights and teachings to help cope with these feelings.

Seeking comfort in the Bible provides redemption and solace to individuals experiencing negative emotions in several ways:

1. Validation and Understanding: The Bible acknowledges the reality of negative emotions, portraying stories of individuals facing hardships, grief, anger, and despair. Validating the depth and range of human emotions through the depiction of stories of individuals who faced similar struggles, offers empathy and understanding. Through the study and repetition of the scripture passages that follow, please know that your feelings are both acknowledged and not uncommon.

2. .Guidance and Wisdom: The Bible offers guidance and wisdom for coping with negative emotions. It provides practical advice on managing emotions such as anger, anxiety, grief, and despair, offering insights on how to navigate these feelings in a healthy and constructive manner. Psalm 34:18 assures, "The Lord is close to the brokenhearted and saves those who are crushed in spirit." The Bible encourages individuals to turn to prayer as a means of finding solace during times of distress. Philippians 4:6 advises, "Do not be anxious about anything, but in every situation, by prayer and petition, with thanksgiving, present your requests to God." Seeking comfort in the Bible encourages individuals to engage in prayer, reflection, and meditation. These practices provide opportunities for self-reflection, introspection, and seeking guidance from God, fostering inner peace and comfort.

3. Promoting Healing and Forgiveness: Through its teachings on forgiveness and reconciliation, the Bible offers a path toward healing for those experiencing emotional pain. It emphasizes the importance of forgiving others and oneself,

allowing for the restoration of inner peace and emotional well-being. Ephesians 4:26 advises, "In your anger, do not sin," encouraging individuals to address anger constructively and avoid letting it lead to wrongdoing.

4.   Internalizing Truths: Repeatedly meditating on comforting scriptures allows individuals to internalize the truths they convey. This process helps ingrain these positive messages into one's thoughts and beliefs, guiding their perspective and responses to negative emotions.

5.   Finding Peace Amidst Anxiety: The Bible provides reassurance and guidance for managing anxiety. Philippians 4:7 promises, "And the peace of God, which transcends all understanding, will guard your hearts and your minds in Christ Jesus."

6.   Overcoming Loneliness: For those experiencing loneliness, the Bible offers the assurance of God's companionship. Hebrews 13:5 reaffirms, "Never will I leave you; never will I forsake you."

7.   Seeking Wisdom in Times of Despair: In moments of despair, the Bible provides wisdom and guidance. Proverbs 3:5-6 advises, "Trust in the Lord with all your heart and lean not on your own understanding; in all your ways submit to him, and he will make your paths straight."

8.   Encouragement During Regret: For those grappling with regret, the Bible emphasizes the importance of seeking forgiveness and moving forward. 1 John 1:9 assures, "If we confess our sins, he is faithful and just and will forgive us our sins and purify us from all unrighteousness."

9.   Comfort Through Stories of Redemption: The Bible showcases stories of redemption, highlighting individuals who found hope and renewal despite their struggles and past mistakes. This provides comfort and encouragement for those facing similar challenges.

10. Promoting Compassion and Love: Above all, the Bible emphasizes compassion, love, and empathy. It encourages individuals to treat others with kindness and understanding, fostering an environment of support and care for those experiencing negative emotions.

11. Assurance of God's Presence: The Bible reassures individuals of God's constant presence and companionship. Scriptures affirm that God is near to the brokenhearted, offering comfort and support to those experiencing emotional distress.

12. Promoting Compassion and Love: Seeking comfort in the Bible fosters a sense of compassion and empathy toward oneself and others. It encourages individuals to treat themselves and those around them with kindness, understanding, and love, creating a supportive environment for emotional healing and comfort.

13. Shifting Focus: Repeating biblical scriptures helps shift one's focus from negative thoughts or emotions to positive and uplifting messages. By dwelling on the comforting words of the Bible, individuals redirect their attention away from distressing feelings, fostering a more positive mindset.

14. Building Faith and Trust: Consistent repetition of comforting scriptures strengthens one's faith and trust in God. It reinforces the belief in God's faithfulness, goodness, and ability to bring comfort and resolution to difficult situations, fostering a sense of hope and peace.

15. Promoting Calmness and Relaxation: Reciting comforting biblical verses can have a calming effect on the mind and body. It encourages deep breathing, relaxation, and a sense of tranquility, reducing the intensity of negative emotions such as anxiety or stress.

16. Empowering Coping Mechanisms: Comforting scriptures often offer practical advice and guidance for coping with challenging emotions. Regular repetition of these verses helps individuals internalize these coping mechanisms, providing

them with effective tools to manage negative emotions.

17. Creating a Source of Strength: Repeatedly engaging with comforting scriptures creates a reservoir of strength and encouragement. During times of emotional distress, individuals can draw upon these verses as a source of spiritual and emotional support, finding strength in the words of the Bible.

Overall, seeking comfort in the Bible provides a framework for understanding, coping with, and transcending negative emotions. It offers a path toward healing, redemption, and emotional well-being by providing guidance, assurance, hope, and the promise of God's unfailing love and presence. And repeating comforting biblical scriptures serves as a powerful tool for managing and alleviating negative emotions by offering affirmation, shifting focus, building faith, internalizing positive truths, promoting calmness, empowering coping strategies, and creating a reliable source of strength and encouragement.

What follows on these pages are hundreds of scriptures for dealing with negative emotions. Each powerful emotion has its own section of the book with supporting scriptures to help overcome and heal.

Peace be with you, my friend.

PART ONE: ANGER

ABOUT ANGER

Anger, a powerful emotion often arising from frustration, hurt, or injustice, can lead to conflict, resentment, and distress. The Bible addresses anger and offers guidance, wisdom, and comfort to those grappling with its effects.

The Bible acknowledges the reality of anger but warns against its destructive potential. Ephesians 4:26-27 advises, "In your anger, do not sin: Do not let the sun go down while you are still angry, and do not give the devil a foothold." This verse recognizes the existence of anger but cautions against allowing it to fester or lead to sin, emphasizing the importance of managing and resolving anger in a timely manner.

Moreover, the Bible provides practical counsel on dealing with anger by promoting forgiveness and reconciliation. Colossians 3:13 urges believers, "Bear with each other and forgive one another if any of you has a grievance against someone. Forgive as the Lord forgave you." This passage encourages individuals to practice forgiveness, allowing for healing and the restoration of relationships affected by anger.

Furthermore, the Bible emphasizes the virtue of patience and self-control in managing anger. Proverbs 29:11 states, "Fools give full vent to their rage, but the wise bring calm in the end." This verse underscores the importance of maintaining composure and exercising self-control when faced with anger, advocating for a measured and thoughtful response rather than reacting impulsively.

Additionally, the Bible provides examples and teachings about the importance of peace and harmony. Romans 12:18 encourages believers, saying, "If it is possible, as far as it depends on you, live at peace with everyone." This verse promotes the pursuit of peace and reconciliation, suggesting that it's crucial to prioritize peace and strive for resolution, even in situations that evoke anger.

Ultimately, the Bible provides comfort to individuals experiencing anger by offering guidance on managing it responsibly, advocating for forgiveness and reconciliation, promoting patience and self-control, and emphasizing the pursuit of peace. It encourages individuals to address anger constructively, guiding them toward reconciliation, healing, and the restoration of peace within themselves and in their relationships.

In your anger, do not sin: Do not let the sun go down while
you are still angry, and do not give the devil a foothold.
Ephesians 4:26-27

My dear brothers and sisters, take note of this:
Everyone should be quick to listen, slow to speak,
and slow to become angry because human anger does
not produce the righteousness that God desires.
James 1:19-20

Fools give full vent to their rage, but the
wise bring calm in the end.
Proverbs 29:11

But now you must also rid yourselves of all such
things as these: anger, rage, malice, slander,
and filthy language from your lips.
Colossians 3:8

Whoever is patient has great understanding, but
one who is quick-tempered displays folly.
Proverbs 14:29

Refrain from anger and turn from wrath;
do not fret—it leads only to evil.
Psalm 37:8

A gentle answer turns away wrath, but
a harsh word stirs up anger.
Proverbs 15:1

Do not be quickly provoked in your spirit,
for anger resides in the lap of fools.
Ecclesiastes 7:9

But I tell you that anyone who is angry with a brother or
sister will be subject to judgment. Again, anyone who says
to a brother or sister, 'Raca,' is answerable to the court. And
anyone who says, 'You fool!' will be in danger of the fire of hell.
Matthew 5:22

Better a patient person than a warrior, one with
self-control than one who takes a city.
Proverbs 16:32

What causes fights and quarrels among you? Don't
they come from your desires that battle within you?
You desire but do not have, so you kill. You covet but
you cannot get what you want, so you quarrel and
fight. You do not have because you do not ask God.
James 4:1-2

A person's wisdom yields patience; it is to
one's glory to overlook an offense.
Proverbs 19:11

Do not make friends with a hot-tempered person,
do not associate with one easily angered, or you may
learn their ways and get yourself ensnared.
Proverbs 22:24-25

The acts of the flesh are obvious: sexual immorality,
impurity, and debauchery; idolatry and witchcraft;
hatred, discord, jealousy, fits of rage, selfish ambition,
dissensions, factions, and envy; drunkenness, orgies,
and the like. I warn you, as I did before, that those who
live like this will not inherit the kingdom of God.
Galatians 5:19-21

An angry person stirs up conflict, and a hot-
tempered person commits many sins.
Proverbs 29:22

Do not take revenge, my dear friends, but leave
room for God's wrath, for it is written: 'It is mine
to avenge; I will repay,' says the Lord.
Romans 12:19

Get rid of all bitterness, rage, and anger, brawling,
and slander, along with every form of malice. Be
kind and compassionate to one another, forgiving
each other, just as in Christ God forgave you.
Ephesians 4:31-32

Tremble and do not sin; when you are on your
beds, search your hearts and be silent.
Psalm 4:4

Since an overseer manages God's household, he must be
blameless—not overbearing, not quick-tempered, not given
to drunkenness, not violent, not pursuing dishonest gain.
Titus 1:7

For as churning cream produces butter, and as twisting the
nose produces blood, so stirring up anger produces strife.
Proverbs 30:33

A hot-tempered person stirs up conflict, but
the one who is patient calms a quarrel.
Proverbs 15:18

Therefore, I want the men everywhere to pray, lifting
up holy hands without anger or disputing.
1 Timothy 2:8

Human anger does not produce the
righteousness that God desires.
James 1:20

A hot-tempered person must pay the penalty;
rescue them, and you will have to do it again.
Proverbs 19:19

Be still before the Lord and wait patiently for him; do
not fret when people succeed in their ways, when they
carry out their wicked schemes. Refrain from anger and
turn from wrath; do not fret—it leads only to evil.
Psalm 37:7-8

Brothers and sisters, do not slander one another. Anyone
who speaks against a brother or sister or judges them
speaks against the law and judges it. When you judge the
law, you are not keeping it, but sitting in judgment on it.
James 4:11

The Lord is gracious and compassionate,
slow to anger and rich in love.
Psalm 145:8

Fools show their annoyance at once, but
the prudent overlook an insult.
Proverbs 12:16

But because of your stubbornness and your unrepentant
heart, you are storing up wrath against yourself for the day of
God's wrath, when his righteous judgment will be revealed.
Romans 2:5

Mockers stir up a city, but the wise turn away anger.
Proverbs 29:8

And the Lord's servant must not be quarrelsome but must
be kind to everyone, able to teach, not resentful. Opponents
must be gently instructed, in the hope that God will grant
them repentance leading them to a knowledge of the truth,
and that they will come to their senses and escape from the
trap of the devil, who has taken them captive to do his will.
2 Timothy 2:24-26

Do not repay anyone evil for evil. Be careful to do what is right
in the eyes of everyone. If it is possible, as far as it depends
on you, live at peace with everyone. Do not take revenge,
my dear friends, but leave room for God's wrath, for it is
written: 'It is mine to avenge; I will repay,' says the Lord.
Romans 12:17-19

A quick-tempered person does foolish things, and
the one who devises evil schemes is hated.
Proverbs 14:17

For where you have envy and selfish ambition,
there you find disorder and every evil practice.
James 3:16

Better to live in a desert than with a
quarrelsome and nagging wife.
Proverbs 21:19

David said to Abigail, 'Praise be to the Lord, the God of Israel, who has sent you today to meet me. May you be blessed for your good judgment and for keeping me from bloodshed this day and from avenging myself with my own hands. Otherwise, as surely as the Lord, the God of Israel, lives, who has kept me from harming you, if you had not come quickly to meet me, not one male belonging to Nabal would have been left alive by daybreak.'
1 Samuel 25:32-34

These passages from the Bible offer guidance and wisdom on managing anger, avoiding conflict, and seeking peace through patience, forgiveness, and self-control.

PART TWO: ANXIETY

ABOUT ANXIETY

Anxiety, characterized by worry, unease, and fear about future uncertainties, can deeply impact individuals' mental and emotional well-being. The Bible acknowledges the reality of anxiety and provides guidance, comfort, and assurance to those experiencing its grip.

One of the fundamental messages the Bible offers to combat anxiety is the call to trust in God's provision and care. Philippians 4:6-7 advises, "Do not be anxious about anything, but in every situation, by prayer and petition, with thanksgiving, present your requests to God. And the peace of God, which transcends all understanding, will guard your hearts and your minds in Christ Jesus." This passage encourages believers to turn to prayer and to bring their concerns and worries to God, promising that His peace will guard their hearts and minds.

Moreover, the Bible emphasizes the importance of focusing on the present moment rather than dwelling on anxious thoughts about the future. In Matthew 6:34, Jesus teaches, "Therefore do not worry about tomorrow, for tomorrow will worry about itself. Each day has enough trouble of its own." This teaching underscores the significance of living in the present and entrusting the future to God's care.

Furthermore, the Bible offers the reassurance of God's presence and His promise to provide strength in times of anxiety. Isaiah 41:10 declares, "So do not fear, for I am with you; do not be dismayed, for I am your God. I will strengthen you and help you; I will uphold you with my righteous right hand." This verse serves as a source of comfort, reminding individuals that God offers His strength and support during times of distress.

Additionally, the Bible encourages believers to cast their anxieties upon God, knowing that He cares for them. 1 Peter 5:7 states, "Cast all your anxiety on him because he cares for you." This verse highlights the importance of surrendering worries to God, trusting in His care and love.

The Bible provides comfort to those experiencing anxiety by encouraging trust in God's provision, emphasizing the importance of prayer and living in the present, assuring believers of God's presence and strength, and reminding individuals of God's care and concern for them. It offers a framework for finding peace amid anxiety by fostering reliance on God's love and guidance.

Do not be anxious about anything, but in every
situation, by prayer and petition, with thanksgiving,
present your requests to God. And the peace of God,
which transcends all understanding, will guard
your hearts and your minds in Christ Jesus.
Philippians 4:6-7

Therefore I tell you, do not worry about your life, what you
will eat or drink; or about your body, what you will wear. Is
not life more than food, and the body more than clothes?
Matthew 6:25

Cast your cares on the Lord and he will sustain
you; he will never let the righteous be shaken.
Psalm 55:22

Therefore do not worry about tomorrow, for tomorrow will
worry about itself. Each day has enough trouble of its own.
Matthew 6:34

When anxiety was great within me, your
consolation brought me joy.
Psalm 94:19

Who of you by worrying can add a single hour to your life?
Luke 12:25

Anxiety weighs down the heart, but a kind word cheers it up.
Proverbs 12:25

Come to me, all you who are weary and burdened, and I will
give you rest. Take my yoke upon you and learn from me,
for I am gentle and humble in heart, and you will find rest
for your souls. For my yoke is easy and my burden is light.
Matthew 11:28-30

Even though I walk through the darkest valley,
I will fear no evil, for you are with me; your
rod and your staff, they comfort me.
Psalm 23:4

Have I not commanded you? Be strong and courageous.
Do not be afraid; do not be discouraged, for the Lord
your God will be with you wherever you go.
Joshua 1:9

I sought the Lord, and he answered me;
he delivered me from all my fears.
Psalm 34:4

I have told you these things, so that in me you may
have peace. In this world, you will have trouble.
But take heart! I have overcome the world.
John 16:33

So we say with confidence, 'The Lord is my helper; I will
not be afraid. What can mere mortals do to me?'
Hebrews 13:6

The Lord is my light and my salvation—whom shall I fear? The
Lord is the stronghold of my life—of whom shall I be afraid?
Psalm 27:1

And my God will meet all your needs according
to the riches of his glory in Christ Jesus.
Philippians 4:19

Can any one of you by worrying add a single hour to your life?
Matthew 6:27

The Lord is with me; I will not be afraid.
What can mere mortals do to me?
Psalm 118:6

Say to those with fearful hearts, 'Be strong, do not
fear; your God will come, he will come with vengeance;
with divine retribution, he will come to save you.'
Isaiah 35:4

May the God of hope fill you with all joy and peace
as you trust in him, so that you may overflow
with hope by the power of the Holy Spirit.
Romans 15:13

Let us then approach God's throne of grace with
confidence, so that we may receive mercy and
find grace to help us in our time of need.
Hebrews 4:16

Commit your way to the Lord; trust in him, and he will act.
Psalm 37:5

Do not conform to the pattern of this world, but be
transformed by the renewing of your mind. Then
you will be able to test and approve what God's
will is—his good, pleasing and perfect will.
Romans 12:2

I lift up my eyes to the mountains—where does
my help come from? My help comes from the
Lord, the Maker of heaven and earth.
Psalm 121:1-2

Consider it pure joy, my brothers and sisters, whenever
you face trials of many kinds because you know that
the testing of your faith produces perseverance.
Let perseverance finish its work so that you may be
mature and complete, not lacking anything.
James 1:2-4

He says, 'Be still, and know that I am God; I will be exalted
among the nations, I will be exalted in the earth.'
Psalm 46:10

And we know that in all things God works for the good of those
who love him, who have been called according to his purpose.
Romans 8:28

Finally, brothers and sisters, whatever is true, whatever
is noble, whatever is right, whatever is pure, whatever
is lovely, whatever is admirable—if anything is excellent
or praiseworthy—think about such things.
Philippians 4:8

The Lord is my shepherd, I lack nothing.
Psalm 23:1

Do not let your hearts be troubled. You
believe in God; believe also in me.
John 14:1

Be still before the Lord and wait patiently for him;
do not fret when people succeed in their ways,
when they carry out their wicked schemes.
Psalm 37:7

Let your gentleness be evident to all. The Lord is near. Do not
be anxious about anything, but in every situation, by prayer
and petition, with thanksgiving, present your requests to God.
Philippians 4:5-6

The Lord will keep you from all harm—He will
watch over your life; the Lord will watch over your
coming and going both now and forevermore.
Psalm 121:7-8

For the Spirit God gave us does not make us timid,
but gives us power, love, and self-discipline.
2 Timothy 1:7

Keep your lives free from the love of money and be
content with what you have, because God has said,
'Never will I leave you; never will I forsake you.' So,
we say with confidence, 'The Lord is my helper; I will
not be afraid. What can mere mortals do to me?'
Hebrews 13:5-6

I am not saying this because I am in need, for I have learned
to be content whatever the circumstances. I know what it
is to be in need, and I know what it is to have plenty. I have
learned the secret of being content in any and every situation,
whether well fed or hungry, whether living in plenty or in
want. I can do all this through him who gives me strength.
Philippians 4:11-13

Trust in the Lord forever, for the Lord, the
Lord himself, is the Rock eternal.
Isaiah 26:4

These verses offer guidance, comfort, and encouragement to those experiencing anxiety, reminding them of God's presence, care, and the promise of peace in difficult times.

PART THREE: DESPAIR

ABOUT DESPAIR

Despair, a state of utter hopelessness or despondency, can overwhelm individuals in moments of deep distress or adversity. In the face of despair, the Bible offers profound solace, hope, and guidance to those experiencing the depths of hopelessness.

Throughout the Scriptures, there are numerous instances where individuals faced seemingly insurmountable challenges and found comfort and restoration through their faith in God. One of the recurring themes in the Bible is the promise of God's presence and His ability to bring hope in the midst of despair. Psalm 34:17-18 affirms this, stating, "The righteous cry out, and the Lord hears them; he delivers them from all their troubles. The Lord is close to the brokenhearted and saves those who are crushed in spirit." This passage serves as a reminder that even in moments of deepest despair, God remains near to provide comfort and rescue.

Moreover, the Bible offers stories of individuals who encountered despair but found restoration through God's intervention. The account of Job, who faced unimaginable loss and suffering, exemplifies this. Despite his despair, Job remained faithful, and in the end, he was restored and blessed abundantly. This narrative serves as an encouragement that even in the depths of despair, there is a possibility of restoration through faith and perseverance.

Additionally, the Bible provides promises of hope and renewal, assuring individuals that despair is not the end of the story. In Isaiah 40:31, it states, "But those who hope in the Lord will renew their strength. They will soar on wings like eagles; they will run and not grow weary, they will walk and not be faint." This verse offers assurance that placing trust in God can bring about renewal and strength, even in the most despairing circumstances.

Furthermore, the Bible emphasizes the importance of seeking God's presence and turning to Him in moments of despair. Psalm 42:11 encourages believers, saying, "Why, my soul, are you downcast? Why so disturbed within me? Put your hope in God, for I will yet praise him, my Savior and my God." This verse underscores the act of consciously placing trust in God and finding hope in His saving grace.

Ultimately, the Bible provides profound comfort to those experiencing despair by assuring them of God's nearness, offering stories of restoration and hope amidst adversity, providing promises of renewal, and encouraging individuals to find solace in God's presence. It instills the belief that even in the darkest moments of despair, there is the possibility of finding hope and restoration through unwavering faith in God.

Why, my soul, are you downcast? Why so disturbed
within me? Put your hope in God, for I will
yet praise him, my Savior and my God.
Psalm 42:11

Yet this I call to mind and therefore I have hope:
Because of the Lord's great love we are not
consumed, for his compassions never fail. They are
new every morning; great is your faithfulness.
Lamentations 3:21-23

We are hard pressed on every side, but not crushed;
perplexed, but not in despair; persecuted, but not
abandoned; struck down, but not destroyed.
2 Corinthians 4:8-9

I wait for the Lord, my whole being waits,
and in his word, I put my hope.
Psalm 130:5

You are my refuge and my shield; I have
put my hope in your word.
Psalm 119:114

And hope does not put us to shame because God's
love has been poured out into our hearts through
the Holy Spirit, who has been given to us.
Romans 5:5

For in this hope we were saved. But hope that is seen is no
hope at all. Who hopes for what they already have? But if we
hope for what we do not yet have, we wait for it patiently.
Romans 8:24-25

We have this hope as an anchor for the soul, firm and
secure. It enters the inner sanctuary behind the curtain.
Hebrews 6:19

Praise be to the God and Father of our Lord Jesus Christ! In
his great mercy, he has given us new birth into a living hope
through the resurrection of Jesus Christ from the dead.
1 Peter 1:3

The righteous cry out, and the Lord hears them; he delivers
them from all their troubles. The Lord is close to the
brokenhearted and saves those who are crushed in spirit.
Psalm 34:17-18

Let us hold unswervingly to the hope we
profess, for he who promised is faithful.
Hebrews 10:23

May your unfailing love be with us, Lord,
even as we put our hope in you.
Psalm 33:22

But God will never forget the needy; the hope
of the afflicted will never perish.
Psalm 9:18

The Spirit of the Sovereign Lord is on me because the Lord
has anointed me to proclaim good news to the poor. He has
sent me to bind up the brokenhearted, to proclaim freedom
for the captives and release from darkness for the prisoners.
Isaiah 61:1

Blessed are those whose help is the God of Jacob,
whose hope is in the Lord their God.
Psalm 146:5

Be strong and take heart, all you who hope in the Lord.
Psalm 31:24

We wait in hope for the Lord; he is our help and our shield.
Psalm 33:20

Be joyful in hope, patient in affliction, faithful in prayer.
Romans 12:12

For everything that was written in the past was written to teach
us, so that through the endurance taught in the Scriptures
and the encouragement they provide, we might have hope.
Romans 15:4

Israel, put your hope in the Lord, for with the Lord is
unfailing love and with him is full redemption.
Psalm 130:7

He gives strength to the weary and
increases the power of the weak.
Isaiah 40:29

But the eyes of the Lord are on those who fear him,
on those whose hope is in his unfailing love.
Psalm 33:18

Now faith is confidence in what we hope for
and assurance about what we do not see.
Hebrews 11:1

I wait for the Lord, my whole being waits, and in his word, I
put my hope. I wait for the Lord more than watchmen wait
for the morning, more than watchmen wait for the morning.
Psalm 130:5-6

Remember your word to your servant,
for you have given me hope.
Psalm 119:49

How abundant are the good things that you have
stored up for those who fear you, that you bestow in
the sight of all, on those who take refuge in you.
Psalm 31:19

You, Lord, hear the desire of the afflicted; you
encourage them, and you listen to their cry.
Psalm 10:17

You will keep in perfect peace those whose minds
are steadfast because they trust in you.
Isaiah 26:3

Why, my soul, are you downcast? Why so disturbed
within me? Put your hope in God, for I will
yet praise him, my Savior and my God.
Psalm 42:5

May those who fear you rejoice when they see
me, for I have put my hope in your word.
Psalm 119:74

Even youths grow tired and weary, and young men stumble
and fall; but those who hope in the Lord will renew their
strength. They will soar on wings like eagles; they will run
and not grow weary, they will walk and not be faint.
Isaiah 40:30-31

In that day they will say, 'Surely this is our God; we trusted
in him, and he saved us. This is the Lord, we trusted
in him; let us rejoice and be glad in his salvation.'
Isaiah 25:9

If you, Lord, kept a record of sins, Lord, who could
stand? But with you there is forgiveness, so that we
can, with reverence, serve you. I wait for the Lord, my
whole being waits, and in his word, I put my hope.
Psalm 130:3-5

Kings will be your foster fathers, and their queens
your nursing mothers. They will bow down before you
with their faces to the ground; they will lick the dust
at your feet. Then you will know that I am the Lord;
those who hope in me will not be disappointed.
Isaiah 49:23

Do not put your trust in princes, in
human beings, who cannot save.
Psalm 146:3

Who among you fears the Lord and obeys the word of his
servant? Let the one who walks in the dark, who has no
light, trust in the name of the Lord and rely on their God.
Isaiah 50:10

You are my refuge and my shield; I have put my
hope in your word. Away from me, you evildoers,
that I may keep the commands of my God!
Psalm 119:114-115

I waited patiently for the Lord; he turned to me and heard my
cry. He lifted me out of the slimy pit, out of the mud and mire;
he set my feet on a rock and gave me a firm place to stand.
He put a new song in my mouth, a hymn of praise to our God.
Many will see and fear the Lord and put their trust in him.
Psalm 40:1-3

Trust in the Lord and do good; dwell in the land and enjoy
safe pasture. Take delight in the Lord, and he will give you the
desires of your heart. Commit your way to the Lord; trust in
him and he will do this: He will make your righteous reward
shine like the dawn, your vindication like the noonday sun.
Psalm 37:3-6

Yes, my soul, find rest in God; my hope comes
from him. Truly he is my rock and my salvation;
he is my fortress, I will not be shaken.
Psalm 62:5-6

"Then you will call on me and come and pray to me, and
I will listen to you. You will seek me and find me when
you seek me with all your heart. I will be found by you,"
declares the Lord, "and will bring you back from captivity.
I will gather you from all the nations and places where I
have banished you," declares the Lord, "and will bring you
back to the place from which I carried you into exile."
Jeremiah 29:12-14

Though the Bible primarily emphasizes hope, these verses
often address feelings of despair or hopelessness by offering
encouragement, assurance, and the promise of God's presence and
faithfulness.

PART FOUR: FEAR

ABOUT FEAR

Fear, a natural and often intense emotional response to perceived threats or dangers, can be a challenging emotion to navigate. The Bible addresses fear in various forms and situations, offering guidance, reassurance, and comfort to those experiencing it.

Repeatedly, the Bible encourages individuals not to succumb to fear but instead to find strength in their faith. One of the most well-known verses addressing fear is found in Isaiah 41:10, where it says, "So do not fear, for I am with you; do not be dismayed, for I am your God. I will strengthen you and help you; I will uphold you with my righteous right hand." This verse reassures believers that God is present, offering protection and support, even in times of uncertainty or distress.

Moreover, the Bible emphasizes that fear does not originate from God but rather from worldly concerns. In 2 Timothy 1:7, it states, "For God has not given us a spirit of fear, but of power and of love and of a sound mind." This verse underscores the idea that fear is not from God and encourages individuals to rely on God's strength and love to overcome their fears.

Additionally, the Bible provides stories and examples of individuals who faced fear but found courage through their faith. One notable example is the story of David and Goliath in 1 Samuel 17, where David, though facing a daunting adversary, trusted in God's power and defeated Goliath. This narrative serves as a reminder that faith in God can conquer even the most overwhelming fears.

Furthermore, the Bible encourages believers to replace fear with trust in God's providence. In Psalm 56:3, it states, "When I am afraid, I put my trust in you." This verse highlights the importance of turning to God in moments of fear, finding solace and strength in the belief that God is in control and will provide guidance and protection.

The Bible offers comfort when you're experiencing fear by providing reassurance of God's presence, emphasizing that fear is not from Him, encouraging faith over fear, and offering examples of individuals who found courage through their trust in God. It instills a sense of hope and reliance on God's strength, assuring believers that they need not face their fears alone.

So do not fear, for I am with you; do not be dismayed,
for I am your God. I will strengthen you and help you;
I will uphold you with my righteous right hand.
Isaiah 41:10

Have I not commanded you? Be strong and courageous.
Do not be afraid; do not be discouraged, for the Lord
your God will be with you wherever you go.
Joshua 1:9

The Lord is my light and my salvation—whom shall I fear? The
Lord is the stronghold of my life—of whom shall I be afraid?
Psalm 27:1

But now, this is what the Lord says—He who created you,
Jacob, He who formed you, Israel: 'Do not fear, for I have
redeemed you; I have summoned you by name; you are mine.'
Isaiah 43:1

Be strong and courageous. Do not be afraid or terrified
because of them, for the Lord your God goes with
you; he will never leave you nor forsake you.
Deuteronomy 31:6

There is no fear in love. But perfect love drives out
fear because fear has to do with punishment. The
one who fears is not made perfect in love.
1 John 4:18

When I am afraid, I put my trust in you.
Psalm 56:3

Do not be afraid of those who kill the body but
cannot kill the soul. Rather, be afraid of the One
who can destroy both soul and body in hell.
Matthew 10:28

For I am convinced that neither death nor life, neither
angels nor demons, neither the present nor the future,
nor any powers, neither height nor depth, nor anything
else in all creation, will be able to separate us from
the love of God that is in Christ Jesus our Lord.
Romans 8:38-39

He will cover you with his feathers, and under his
wings, you will find refuge; his faithfulness will
be your shield and rampart. You will not fear the
terror of night, nor the arrow that flies by day.
Psalm 91:4-5

For I am the Lord your God who takes hold of your right
hand and says to you, Do not fear; I will help you.
Isaiah 41:13

Fear of man will prove to be a snare, but
whoever trusts in the Lord is kept safe.
Proverbs 29:25

Indeed, the very hairs of your head are all numbered. Don't
be afraid; you are worth more than many sparrows.
Luke 12:7

For the Spirit God gave us does not make us timid,
but gives us power, love, and self-discipline.
2 Timothy 1:7

They will have no fear of bad news; their hearts
are steadfast, trusting in the Lord.
Psalm 112:7

God is our refuge and strength, an ever-present help in
trouble. Therefore we will not fear, though the earth give
way and the mountains fall into the heart of the sea.
Psalm 46:1-2

Do not be afraid; you will not be put to shame. Do
not fear disgrace; you will not be humiliated. You
will forget the shame of your youth and remember
no more the reproach of your widowhood.
Isaiah 54:4

Praise the Lord. Blessed are those who fear the Lord, who find
great delight in his commands. Their children will be mighty
in the land; the generation of the upright will be blessed.
Psalm 112:1-2

You who fear him, trust in the Lord—he is their help and shield.
Psalm 115:11

Do not be afraid, for I am with you; I will bring your
children from the east and gather you from the west.
Isaiah 43:5

But the angel said to her, 'Do not be afraid,
Mary; you have found favor with God.'
Luke 1:30

But even if you should suffer for what is right, you are
blessed. 'Do not fear their threats; do not be frightened.'
1 Peter 3:14

You, dear children, are from God and have
overcome them because the one who is in you is
greater than the one who is in the world.
1 John 4:4

He fulfills the desires of those who fear him;
he hears their cry and saves them.
Psalm 145:19

Do not be afraid, little flock, for your Father has
been pleased to give you the kingdom.
Luke 12:32

Do not tremble, do not be afraid. Did I not proclaim this and
foretell it long ago? You are my witnesses. Is there any God
besides me? No, there is no other Rock; I know not one.
Isaiah 44:8

One night the Lord spoke to Paul in a vision: 'Do not
be afraid; keep on speaking, do not be silent.'
Acts 18:9

When I saw him, I fell at his feet as though dead.
Then he placed his right hand on me and said: 'Do
not be afraid. I am the First and the Last.'
Revelation 1:17

Do not be afraid of what you are about to suffer. I tell you,
the devil will put some of you in prison to test you, and you
will suffer persecution for ten days. Be faithful, even to the
point of death, and I will give you life as your victor's crown.
Revelation 2:10

Overhearing what they said, Jesus told
him, 'Don't be afraid; just believe.'
Mark 5:36

The angel of the Lord encamps around those
who fear him, and he delivers them.
Psalm 34:7

The Lord is with me; he is my helper. I
look in triumph on my enemies.
Psalm 118:7

Their hearts are secure, they will have no fear; in
the end, they will look in triumph on their foes.
Psalm 112:8

But blessed is the one who trusts in the
Lord, whose confidence is in him.
Jeremiah 17:7

Surely God is my salvation; I will trust and not be
afraid. The Lord, the Lord himself, is my strength
and my defense; he has become my salvation.
Isaiah 12:2

Though an army besiege me, my heart will not fear; though
war break out against me, even then I will be confident.
Psalm 27:3

Surely the righteous will never be shaken; they will
be remembered forever. They will have no fear of bad
news; their hearts are steadfast, trusting in the Lord.
Psalm 112:6-7

When you hear of wars and uprisings, do not
be frightened. These things must happen first,
but the end will not come right away.
Luke 21:9

Therefore, since we are receiving a kingdom that
cannot be shaken, let us be thankful, and so worship
God acceptably with reverence and awe.
Hebrews 12:28

And because of my chains, most of the brothers and
sisters have become confident in the Lord and dare
all the more to proclaim the gospel without fear.
Philippians 1:14

The Spirit you received does not make you slaves, so that you
live in fear again; rather, the Spirit you received brought about
your adoption to sonship. And by him, we cry, 'Abba, Father.'
Romans 8:15

These passages offer reassurance, strength, and encouragement
in the face of fear, reminding us of God's presence, protection, and
love.

PART FIVE: GRIEF

ABOUT GRIEF

Grief, an intense emotional response to loss, encompasses various emotions such as sadness, sorrow, and anguish. The Bible addresses grief as a natural part of the human experience, providing solace, guidance, and comfort to those navigating the profound pain of loss.

The scriptures offer empathy and understanding to individuals experiencing grief, acknowledging the depth of their emotions. In John 11:35, one of the shortest yet most profound verses in the Bible, it is noted, "Jesus wept." These two words capture the compassion of Jesus when He witnessed the grief of Mary and Martha after the death of their brother Lazarus. This passage demonstrates that Jesus Himself experienced the sorrow of loss and empathizes with those who mourn.

Furthermore, the Bible assures individuals experiencing grief that they are not alone in their suffering. Psalm 34:18 tenderly affirms, "The Lord is close to the brokenhearted and saves those who are crushed in spirit." This verse offers solace by reminding individuals that God is present during times of deep emotional pain, offering comfort and understanding.

Moreover, the Bible provides hope and assurance of life beyond the sorrow of grief. In 1 Thessalonians 4:13-14, it states, "Brothers and sisters, we do not want you to be uninformed about those who sleep in death so that you do not grieve like the rest of mankind, who have no hope. For we believe that Jesus died and rose again, and so we believe that God will bring with Jesus those who have fallen asleep in him." This passage brings the promise of resurrection and eternal life, offering hope and a perspective that extends beyond the pain of loss.

Additionally, the Bible encourages individuals to find strength in God's love and promises during times of grief. Romans 8:38-39 assures believers that nothing—neither death nor life—can separate them from the love of God. This reminder brings comfort, assuring that even in the midst of pain, God's love remains steadfast and enduring.

Ultimately, the Bible provides profound comfort to those experiencing grief by acknowledging their pain, offering empathetic understanding, assuring them of God's presence, promising hope beyond the sorrow, and emphasizing the enduring love and faithfulness of God during times of profound loss.

The Lord is close to the brokenhearted and
saves those who are crushed in spirit.
Psalm 34:18

He heals the brokenhearted and binds up their wounds.
Psalm 147:3

Blessed are those who mourn, for they will be comforted.
Matthew 5:4

I consider that our present sufferings are not worth
comparing with the glory that will be revealed in us.
Romans 8:18

In the same way, the Spirit helps us in our weakness. We
do not know what we ought to pray for, but the Spirit
himself intercedes for us through wordless groans.
Romans 8:26

Rejoice with those who rejoice; mourn with those who mourn.
Romans 12:15

Praise be to the God and Father of our Lord Jesus Christ,
the Father of compassion and the God of all comfort, who
comforts us in all our troubles, so that we can comfort those in
any trouble with the comfort we ourselves receive from God.
2 Corinthians 1:3-4

In all this you greatly rejoice, though now for a little
while you may have had to suffer grief in all kinds of
trials. These have come so that the proven genuineness
of your faith—of greater worth than gold, which perishes
even though refined by fire—may result in praise,
glory and honor when Jesus Christ is revealed.
1 Peter 1:6-7

For his anger lasts only a moment, but his favor
lasts a lifetime; weeping may stay for the night,
but rejoicing comes in the morning.
Psalm 30:5

Those who sow with tears will reap with songs of joy.
Psalm 126:5

When you pass through the waters, I will be with you;
and when you pass through the rivers, they will not
sweep over you. When you walk through the fire, you
will not be burned; the flames will not set you ablaze.
Isaiah 43:2

Surely he took up our pain and bore our suffering, yet we
considered him punished by God, stricken by him, and
afflicted. But he was pierced for our transgressions, he was
crushed for our iniquities; the punishment that brought
us peace was on him, and by his wounds, we are healed.
Isaiah 53:4-5

For I know the plans I have for you, declares
the Lord, plans to prosper you and not to harm
you, plans to give you hope and a future.
Jeremiah 29:11

For no one is cast off by the Lord forever. Though he brings
grief, he will show compassion, so great is his unfailing love.
For he does not willingly bring affliction or grief to anyone.
Lamentations 3:31-33

Come to me, all you who are weary and burdened, and I will
give you rest. Take my yoke upon you and learn from me,
for I am gentle and humble in heart, and you will find rest
for your souls. For my yoke is easy and my burden is light.
Matthew 11:28-30

So with you: Now is your time of grief, but I will see you again
and you will rejoice, and no one will take away your joy.
John 16:22

Not only so, but we also glory in our sufferings,
because we know that suffering produces perseverance;
perseverance, character; and character, hope.
Romans 5:3-4

Therefore we do not lose heart. Though outwardly we are
wasting away, yet inwardly we are being renewed day by
day. For our light and momentary troubles are achieving
for us an eternal glory that far outweighs them all. So we fix
our eyes not on what is seen, but on what is unseen, since
what is seen is temporary, but what is unseen is eternal.
2 Corinthians 4:16-18

Godly sorrow brings repentance that leads to salvation
and leaves no regret, but worldly sorrow brings death.
2 Corinthians 7:10

And do not grieve the Holy Spirit of God, with whom
you were sealed for the day of redemption.
Ephesians 4:30

I can do all this through him who gives me strength.
Philippians 4:13

Let the peace of Christ rule in your hearts, since as members
of one body you were called to peace. And be thankful.
Colossians 3:15

Therefore encourage one another and build each
other up, just as in fact you are doing.
1 Thessalonians 5:11

For we do not have a high priest who is unable to
empathize with our weaknesses, but we have one who
has been tempted in every way, just as we are—yet
he did not sin. Let us then approach God's throne of
grace with confidence, so that we may receive mercy
and find grace to help us in our time of need.
Hebrews 4:15-16

Fixing our eyes on Jesus, the pioneer, and perfecter of faith.
For the joy set before him, he endured the cross, scorning its
shame, and sat down at the right hand of the throne of God.
Hebrews 12:2

And the God of all grace, who called you to his eternal glory
in Christ, after you have suffered a little while, will himself
restore you and make you strong, firm, and steadfast.
1 Peter 5:10

He will wipe every tear from their eyes. There will
be no more death or mourning or crying or pain,
for the old order of things has passed away.
Revelation 21:4

May your unfailing love be my comfort,
according to your promise to your servant.
Psalm 119:76

You turned my wailing into dancing; you removed
my sackcloth and clothed me with joy.
Psalm 30:11

Then young women will dance and be glad, young men
and old as well. I will turn their mourning into gladness;
I will give them comfort and joy instead of sorrow.
Jeremiah 31:13

Because of the Lord's great love we are not
consumed, for his compassions never fail. They are
new every morning; great is your faithfulness.
Lamentations 3:22-23

He comforts us in all our troubles so that we can
comfort others. When they are troubled, we will be able
to give them the same comfort God has given us.
2 Corinthians 1:4

He sets on high those who are lowly, and
those who mourn are lifted to safety.
Job 5:11

My intercessor is my friend as my eyes pour out tears to God.
Job 16:20

My soul is weary with sorrow; strengthen
me according to your word.
Psalm 119:28

You keep track of all my sorrows. You have collected all my
tears in your bottle. You have recorded each one in your book.
Psalm 56:8

He was despised and rejected by mankind, a man of suffering,
and familiar with pain. Like one from whom people hide
their faces he was despised, and we held him in low esteem.
Isaiah 53:3

Then he said to them, 'My soul is overwhelmed with sorrow
to the point of death. Stay here and keep watch with me.'
Matthew 26:38

"My soul is overwhelmed with sorrow to the point of
death," he said to them. "Stay here and keep watch."
Mark 14:34

But God, who comforts the downcast, comforted us by
the coming of Titus, and not only by his coming but
also by the comfort you had given him. He told us about
your longing for me, your deep sorrow, your ardent
concern for me so that my joy was greater than ever.
2 Corinthians 7:6-7

These passages reflect the Bible's acknowledgment of grief,
providing comfort, hope, and guidance to those experiencing
sorrow and mourning.

PART SIX: JEALOUSY

ABOUT JEALOUSY

Jealousy, a complex and often painful emotion arising from feelings of envy, possessiveness, or insecurity, can deeply affect relationships and one's sense of contentment. The Bible addresses jealousy and provides guidance, wisdom, and comfort to individuals experiencing its tumultuous effects.

The Bible acknowledges the destructiveness of jealousy and the turmoil it can bring to individuals and relationships. James 3:16 warns, "For where you have envy and selfish ambition, there you find disorder and every evil practice." This verse highlights the negative consequences of jealousy, emphasizing its divisive and harmful nature.

Moreover, the Bible offers wisdom and counsel to navigate feelings of jealousy by promoting contentment and gratitude. Hebrews 13:5 encourages believers, stating, "Keep your lives free from the love of money and be content with what you have because God has said, 'Never will I leave you; never will I forsake you.'" This verse suggests that finding contentment and trust in God's provision can counteract feelings of jealousy and discontent.

Furthermore, the Bible promotes love, kindness, and humility as antidotes to jealousy. In 1 Corinthians 13:4-7, known as the "Love Chapter," it describes love as patient, kind, not envious, and not boastful. This passage emphasizes the importance of fostering love and humility, qualities that can help alleviate jealousy and promote healthy relationships.

Additionally, the Bible offers stories that demonstrate the destructive nature of jealousy and its consequences. The story of Cain and Abel in Genesis 4 depicts how jealousy led Cain to commit a grievous act against his brother. This narrative serves as a cautionary tale, illustrating the harmful outcomes of jealousy and envy.

Ultimately, the Bible provides comfort to individuals experiencing jealousy by offering guidance on cultivating contentment, promoting love and humility, and warning against the destructive nature of jealousy. It encourages individuals to focus on gratitude, love, and humility, fostering an environment that mitigates the negative effects of jealousy and promotes healthy relationships.

A heart at peace gives life to the body, but envy rots the bones.
Proverbs 14:30

Let us not become conceited, provoking
and envying each other.
Galatians 5:26

Anger is cruel and fury overwhelming, but
who can stand before jealousy?
Proverbs 27:4

You desire but do not have, so you kill. You covet but
you cannot get what you want, so you quarrel and
fight. You do not have because you do not ask God.
James 4:2

Let us behave decently, as in the daytime, not in
carousing and drunkenness, not in sexual immorality
and debauchery, not in dissension and jealousy.
Romans 13:13

Therefore, rid yourselves of all malice and all deceit,
hypocrisy, envy, and slander of every kind.
1 Peter 2:1

And I saw that all toil and all achievement spring
from one person's envy of another. This too is
meaningless, a chasing after the wind.
Ecclesiastes 4:4

A heart at peace gives life to the body, but envy rots the bones.
Proverbs 14:30

They are conceited and understand nothing. They have an
unhealthy interest in controversies and quarrels about words
that result in envy, strife, malicious talk, evil suspicions.
1 Timothy 6:4

Do not envy the wicked, do not desire their company; for their
hearts plot violence, and their lips talk about making trouble.
Proverbs 24:1-2

When the Jews saw the crowds, they were filled
with jealousy. They began to contradict what
Paul was saying and heaped abuse on him.
Acts 13:45

Do not let your heart envy sinners, but always
be zealous for the fear of the Lord.
Proverbs 23:17

You are still worldly. For since there is jealousy
and quarreling among you, are you not worldly?
Are you not acting like mere humans?
1 Corinthians 3:3

For he knew it was out of self-interest that
they had handed Jesus over to him.
Matthew 27:18

For where you have envy and selfish ambition,
there you find disorder and every evil practice.
James 3:16

Because the patriarchs were jealous of Joseph, they sold
him as a slave into Egypt. But God was with him.
Acts 7:9

Are we trying to arouse the Lord's jealousy?
Are we stronger than he?
1 Corinthians 10:22

But other Jews were jealous; so they rounded
up some bad characters from the marketplace,
formed a mob and started a riot in the city.
Acts 17:5

No one can serve two masters. Either you will hate the one
and love the other, or you will be devoted to the one and
despise the other. You cannot serve both God and money.
Matthew 6:24

His brothers were jealous of him, but his
father kept the matter in mind.
Genesis 37:11

For I envied the arrogant when I saw
the prosperity of the wicked.
Psalm 73:3

But if you harbor bitter envy and selfish ambition
in your hearts, do not boast about it or deny the
truth. Such 'wisdom' does not come down from
heaven but is earthly, unspiritual, demonic.
James 3:14-15

For he knew it was out of self-interest that
they had handed Jesus over to him.
Mark 15:10

For jealousy arouses a husband's fury, and he
will show no mercy when he takes revenge.
Proverbs 6:34

Love is patient, love is kind. It does not envy, it does not boast,
it is not proud. It does not dishonor others, it is not self-
seeking, it is not easily angered, it keeps no record of wrongs.
1 Corinthians 13:4-6

The acts of the flesh are obvious: sexual immorality,
impurity, and debauchery; idolatry and witchcraft;
hatred, discord, jealousy, fits of rage, selfish ambition,
dissensions, factions, and envy; drunkenness, orgies,
and the like. I warn you, as I did before, that those who
live like this will not inherit the kingdom of God.
Galatians 5:19-21

When Rachel saw that she was not bearing Jacob
any children, she became jealous of her sister. So,
she said to Jacob, 'Give me children, or I'll die!
Genesis 30:1

He is conceited and understands nothing. He has an
unhealthy interest in controversies and quarrels about words
that result in envy, strife, malicious talk, evil suspicions.
1 Timothy 6:4

Do not let your heart envy sinners, but always
be zealous for the fear of the Lord.
Proverbs 23:17

But if you harbor bitter envy and selfish ambition in
your hearts, do not boast about it or deny the truth. Such
wisdom does not come down from heaven but is earthly,
unspiritual, demonic. For where you have envy and selfish
ambition, there you find disorder and every evil practice.
James 3:14-16

Wrath is cruel and anger a torrent, but who
is able to stand before jealousy?
Proverbs 27:4

These passages provide insight into jealousy and envy as harmful and sinful behaviors, often resulting in negative consequences and discord among individuals. They serve as cautionary reminders within the Bible about the dangers and disruptive effects of envy and jealousy.

PART SEVEN: LONELINESS

ABOUT LONELINESS

Loneliness, a profound sense of isolation or emotional emptiness often stemming from a lack of companionship or meaningful connections, can deeply affect one's mental and emotional well-being. The Bible addresses loneliness and offers guidance, companionship, and comfort to those experiencing its distressing effects.

The Bible acknowledges the experience of loneliness, portraying various individuals who grappled with isolation or feelings of being forsaken. One notable example is found in Psalm 25:16-17, where the psalmist expresses, "Turn to me and be gracious to me, for I am lonely and afflicted. Relieve the troubles of my heart and free me from my anguish." This heartfelt plea highlights the psalmist's vulnerability and longing for relief from loneliness.

Moreover, the Bible emphasizes the presence and companionship of God as a source of comfort and solace in times of loneliness. Hebrews 13:5 assures believers, "Never will I leave you; never will I forsake you." This verse underscores the unwavering presence of God, offering reassurance that even in moments of isolation, individuals are not truly alone, as God remains with them.

Furthermore, the Bible encourages believers to seek fellowship and community with others. Ecclesiastes 4:9-10 promotes the idea of companionship, stating, "Two are better than one because they have a good return for their labor: If either of them falls down, one can help the other up. But pity anyone who falls and has no one to help them up." This passage underscores the value of mutual support and companionship, highlighting the significance of relationships in combating loneliness.

Additionally, the Bible offers narratives that demonstrate how individuals found companionship and support during periods of loneliness. The story of Ruth and Naomi exemplifies this, showing the companionship and loyalty between these two women during their times of hardship, providing comfort and support to one another.

Ultimately, the Bible provides comfort to those experiencing loneliness by acknowledging their feelings, assuring the presence of God as a constant companion, advocating for fellowship and community, and presenting stories of companionship and support. It encourages individuals to seek connections with others, offering solace and the promise of divine companionship to alleviate the burden of loneliness.

Turn to me and be gracious to me, for I am lonely and afflicted.
Relieve the troubles of my heart and free me from my anguish.
Psalm 25:16-17

God sets the lonely in families; he leads out the prisoners
with singing; but the rebellious live in a sun-scorched land.
Psalm 68:6

Keep your lives free from the love of money and be
content with what you have, because God has said,
'Never will I leave you; never will I forsake you.'
Hebrews 13:5

I will not leave you as orphans; I will come to you.
John 14:18

Be strong and courageous. Do not be afraid or terrified
because of them, for the Lord your God goes with
you; he will never leave you nor forsake you.
Deuteronomy 31:6

And surely I am with you always, to the very end of the age.
Matthew 28:20

Yet I am always with you; you hold me by my right hand. You
guide me with your counsel, and afterward, you will take me
into glory. Whom have I in heaven but you? And earth has
nothing I desire besides you. My flesh and my heart may fail,
but God is the strength of my heart and my portion forever.
Psalm 73:23-26

Where can I go from your Spirit? Where can I flee from your
presence? If I go up to the heavens, you are there; if I make
my bed in the depths, you are there. If I rise on the wings
of the dawn, if I settle on the far side of the sea, even there
your hand will guide me, your right hand will hold me fast.
Psalm 139:7-10

When you pass through the waters, I will be with you;
and when you pass through the rivers, they will not
sweep over you. When you walk through the fire, you
will not be burned; the flames will not set you ablaze.
Isaiah 43:2

No one who hopes in you will ever be put to shame, but shame
will come on those who are treacherous without cause.
Psalm 25:3

Yes, my soul, find rest in God; my hope comes from him. Truly
he is my rock and my salvation; he is my fortress, I will not
be shaken. My salvation and my honor depend on God; he
is my mighty rock, my refuge. Trust in him at all times, you
people; pour out your hearts to him, for God is our refuge.
Psalm 62:5-8

Can a mother forget the baby at her breast and have no
compassion on the child she has borne? Though she may
forget, I will not forget you! See, I have engraved you on
the palms of my hands; your walls are ever before me.
Isaiah 49:15-16

But as for me, I am poor and needy; may the
Lord think of me. You are my help and my
deliverer; you are my God, do not delay.
Psalm 40:17

A father to the fatherless, a defender of widows,
is God in his holy dwelling. God sets the lonely in
families, he leads out the prisoners with singing;
but the rebellious live in a sun-scorched land.
Psalm 68:5-6

But now, this is what the Lord says— he who created you,
Jacob, he who formed you, Israel: 'Do not fear, for I have
redeemed you; I have summoned you by name; you are mine.'
Isaiah 43:1

Do not be afraid, for I am with you; I will bring your
children from the east and gather you from the west.
Isaiah 43:5

No one will be able to stand against you all the days
of your life. As I was with Moses, so I will be with
you; I will never leave you nor forsake you.
Joshua 1:5

Look and see, there is no one at my right hand; no one is
concerned for me. I have no refuge; no one cares for my life.
Psalm 142:4

For we do not have a high priest who is unable to
empathize with our weaknesses, but we have one who
has been tempted in every way, just as we are—yet
he did not sin. Let us then approach God's throne of
grace with confidence, so that we may receive mercy
and find grace to help us in our time of need.
Hebrews 4:15-16

Cast all your anxiety on him because he cares for you.
1 Peter 5:7

Answer me quickly, Lord; my spirit fails. Do not hide
your face from me or I will be like those who go down
to the pit. Let the morning bring me word of your
unfailing love, for I have put my trust in you. Show me
the way I should go, for to you I entrust my life.
Psalm 143:7-8

Truly my soul finds rest in God; my salvation comes
from him. Truly he is my rock and my salvation;
he is my fortress, I will never be shaken.
Psalm 62:1-2

Forget the former things; do not dwell on the past.
See, I am doing a new thing! Now it springs up;
do you not perceive it? I am making a way in the
wilderness and streams in the wasteland.
Isaiah 43:18-19

The Lord confides in those who fear him; he
makes his covenant known to them.
Psalm 25:14

Though my father and mother forsake
me, the Lord will receive me.
Psalm 27:10

So do not fear, for I am with you; do not be dismayed,
for I am your God. I will strengthen you and help you;
I will uphold you with my righteous right hand.
Isaiah 41:10

The Lord your God is with you, the Mighty Warrior who
saves. He will take great delight in you; in his love, he will no
longer rebuke you, but will rejoice over you with singing.
Zephaniah 3:17

I have told you these things, so that in me you may
have peace. In this world, you will have trouble.
But take heart! I have overcome the world.
John 16:33

Peace I leave with you; my peace I give you. I do
not give to you as the world gives. Do not let your
hearts be troubled and do not be afraid.
John 14:27

Come to me, all you who are weary and burdened, and I will
give you rest. Take my yoke upon you and learn from me,
for I am gentle and humble in heart, and you will find rest
for your souls. For my yoke is easy and my burden is light.
Matthew 11:28-30

These passages offer comfort, assurance, and the promise of
God's presence and support for those who may be experiencing
loneliness or feeling isolated. They emphasize God's love, care, and
constant presence in the lives of individuals, bringing hope and
encouragement in times of solitude or distress.

PART EIGHT: POVERTY

ABOUT POVERTY

Poverty, throughout history and across various cultures, has been a pervasive challenge that affects individuals, families, and communities. It encompasses a lack of resources, financial instability, and often leads to hardships in meeting basic needs such as food, shelter, and healthcare. Within the Bible, poverty is a recurrent theme, and the scriptures offer guidance, compassion, and support to those facing such circumstances.

In the biblical text, there is a consistent call for compassion and care for the poor and vulnerable. Jesus Christ Himself emphasized the importance of caring for the less fortunate, encouraging acts of charity and kindness. In Matthew 25:35-36, Jesus said, "For I was hungry and you gave me something to eat, I was thirsty and you gave me something to drink, I was a stranger and you invited me in, I needed clothes and you clothed me, I was sick and you looked after me, I was in prison and you came to visit me." This passage underscores the significance of helping those in need as a reflection of one's relationship with God.

Additionally, the Bible provides comfort and assurance to those experiencing poverty by offering hope and emphasizing God's presence in their lives. Verses such as Psalm 34:10, which states, "The lions may grow weak and hungry, but those who seek the Lord lack no good thing," serve as a reminder that seeking God can bring fulfillment even in times of scarcity. Psalm 9:18 also affirms this, stating, "But God will never forget the needy; the hope of the afflicted will never perish."

Moreover, the Bible often highlights the blessings that come to those who are generous and caring toward the poor. Proverbs 19:17 declares, "Whoever is kind to the poor lends to the Lord, and he will reward them for what they have done." This notion reinforces the idea that acts of kindness towards those in poverty are seen as honorable and are rewarded in the eyes of God.

While the Bible acknowledges the existence of poverty and the challenges it brings, it also emphasizes the importance of compassion, generosity, and hope. It encourages individuals to care for one another and to trust in God's provision, offering comfort and guidance to both those experiencing poverty and those seeking to support and uplift them.

Whoever oppresses the poor shows contempt for their
Maker, but whoever is kind to the needy honors God.
Proverbs 14:31

Whoever is kind to the poor lends to the Lord, and
he will reward them for what they have done.
Proverbs 19:17

Whoever shuts their ears to the cry of the poor
will also cry out and not be answered.
Proverbs 21:13

Rich and poor have this in common: The
Lord is the Maker of them all.
Proverbs 22:2

The generous will themselves be blessed, for
they share their food with the poor.
Proverbs 22:9

Those who give to the poor will lack nothing, but those
who close their eyes to them receive many curses.
Proverbs 28:27

Defend the weak and the fatherless; uphold the cause
of the poor and the oppressed. Rescue the weak and the
needy; deliver them from the hand of the wicked.
Psalm 82:3-4

For you have been a refuge to the poor, a refuge
to the needy in their distress, a shelter from
the storm and a shade from the heat.
Isaiah 25:4

The poor and needy search for water, but there is none;
their tongues are parched with thirst. But I the Lord will
answer them; I, the God of Israel, will not forsake them.
Isaiah 41:17

Is not this the kind of fasting I have chosen: to loose the
chains of injustice and untie the cords of the yoke, to set
the oppressed free and break every yoke? Is it not to share
your food with the hungry and to provide the poor wanderer
with shelter—when you see the naked, to clothe them,
and not to turn away from your own flesh and blood?
Isaiah 58:6-7

He defended the cause of the poor and needy, and so all went
well. Is that not what it means to know me? declares the Lord.
Jeremiah 22:16

Now this was the sin of your sister Sodom: She
and her daughters were arrogant, overfed and
unconcerned; they did not help the poor and needy.
Ezekiel 16:49

Do not oppress the widow or the fatherless, the foreigner
or the poor. Do not plot evil against each other.
Zechariah 7:10

Blessed are the poor in spirit, for theirs
is the kingdom of heaven.
Matthew 5:3

Jesus answered, 'If you want to be perfect, go, sell
your possessions and give to the poor, and you will
have treasure in heaven. Then come, follow me.'
Matthew 19:21

Then the King will say to those on his right, 'Come, you
who are blessed by my Father; take your inheritance,
the kingdom prepared for you since the creation of the
world. For I was hungry and you gave me something
to eat, I was thirsty and you gave me something to
drink, I was a stranger and you invited me in, I needed
clothes and you clothed me, I was sick and you looked
after me, I was in prison and you came to visit me.'
Matthew 25:34-36

John answered, 'Anyone who has two shirts
should share with the one who has none, and
anyone who has food should do the same.'
Luke 3:11

Looking at his disciples, he said: 'Blessed are you who
are poor, for yours is the kingdom of God. Blessed
are you who hunger now, for you will be satisfied.
Blessed are you who weep now, for you will laugh.'
Luke 6:20-21

Sell your possessions and give to the poor. Provide purses for
yourselves that will not wear out, a treasure in heaven that will
never fail, where no thief comes near and no moth destroys.
For where your treasure is, there your heart will be also.
Luke 12:33-34

But when you give a banquet, invite the poor,
the crippled, the lame, the blind, and you will be
blessed. Although they cannot repay you, you will
be repaid at the resurrection of the righteous.
Luke 14:13-14

In everything I did, I showed you that by this kind of hard
work we must help the weak, remembering the words the Lord
Jesus himself said: 'It is more blessed to give than to receive.'
Acts 20:35

Share with the Lord's people who are
in need. Practice hospitality.
Romans 12:13

If I give all I possess to the poor and give over my body to
hardship that I may boast, but do not have love, I gain nothing.
1 Corinthians 13:3

All they asked was that we should continue to remember
the poor, the very thing I had been eager to do all along.
Galatians 2:10

Religion that God our Father accepts as pure and faultless
is this: to look after orphans and widows in their distress
and to keep oneself from being polluted by the world.
James 1:27

Listen, my dear brothers and sisters: Has not God chosen
those who are poor in the eyes of the world to be rich in faith
and to inherit the kingdom he promised those who love him?
James 2:5

Suppose a brother or a sister is without clothes
and daily food. If one of you says to them, 'Go in
peace; keep warm and well fed,' but does nothing
about their physical needs, what good is it?
James 2:15-16

Now listen, you rich people, weep and wail because of the
misery that is coming on you. Your wealth has rotted, and
moths have eaten your clothes. Your gold and silver are
corroded. Their corrosion will testify against you and eat
your flesh like fire. You have hoarded wealth in the last
days. Look! The wages you failed to pay the workers who
mowed your fields are crying out against you. The cries of
the harvesters have reached the ears of the Lord Almighty.
You have lived on earth in luxury and self-indulgence.
You have fattened yourselves in the day of slaughter.
James 5:1-5

If anyone has material possessions and sees a
brother or sister in need but has no pity on them,
how can the love of God be in that person?
1 John 3:17

If anyone is poor among your fellow Israelites in any of
the towns of the land the Lord your God is giving you,
do not be hardhearted or tightfisted toward them.
Deuteronomy 15:7

There will always be poor people in the land. Therefore
I command you to be openhanded toward your fellow
Israelites who are poor and needy in your land.
Deuteronomy 15:11

Blessed are those who have regard for the weak;
the Lord delivers them in times of trouble.
Psalm 41:1

For he will deliver the needy who cry out,
the afflicted who have no one to help.
Psalm 72:12

For he stands at the right hand of the needy, to save
their lives from those who would condemn them.
Psalm 109:31

The righteous care about justice for the poor,
but the wicked have no such concern.
Proverbs 29:7

Woe to those who make unjust laws, to those who issue
oppressive decrees, to deprive the poor of their rights
and withhold justice from the oppressed of my people,
making widows their prey and robbing the fatherless.
Isaiah 10:1-2

Is it not to share your food with the hungry and to provide the
poor wanderer with shelter—when you see the naked, to clothe
them, and not to turn away from your own flesh and blood?
Isaiah 58:7

They have grown fat and sleek. Their evil deeds have no limit;
they do not seek justice. They do not promote the case of the
fatherless; they do not defend the just cause of the poor.
Jeremiah 5:28

This is what the Lord says: Do what is just and right. Rescue
from the hand of the oppressor the one who has been robbed.
Do no wrong or violence to the foreigner, the fatherless or
the widow, and do not shed innocent blood in this place.
Jeremiah 22:3

This is what the Lord says: 'For three sins of Israel,
even for four, I will not relent. They sell the innocent
for silver, and the needy for a pair of sandals. They
trample on the heads of the poor as on the dust of
the ground and deny justice to the oppressed.'
Amos 2:6-7

He has shown you, O mortal, what is good. And what
does the Lord require of you? To act justly and to
love mercy and to walk humbly with your God.
Micah 6:8

The blind receive sight, the lame walk, those who have
leprosy are cleansed, the deaf hear, the dead are raised,
and the good news is proclaimed to the poor.
Matthew 11:5

Jesus looked at him and loved him. 'One thing you lack,' he
said. 'Go, sell everything you have and give to the poor, and
you will have treasure in heaven. Then come, follow me.'
Mark 10:21

He has filled the hungry with good things
but has sent the rich away empty.
Luke 1:53

But woe to you who are rich, for you have
already received your comfort.
Luke 6:24

These passages reflect the Bible's emphasis on caring for
the poor, seeking justice, and demonstrating compassion and
generosity toward those in need.

PART NINE: REGRET

ABOUT REGRET

Regret, a poignant feeling of sadness or disappointment over past actions or choices, can weigh heavily on individuals, leading to emotional distress and longing for a different outcome. The Bible addresses regret and offers guidance, forgiveness, and hope to those burdened by feelings of remorse.

The Bible acknowledges the reality of regret and its impact on individuals. It showcases various figures who experienced regret over their actions, such as King David, who deeply regretted his affair with Bathsheba and the subsequent consequences. In Psalm 51:10, David expresses his remorse, pleading, "Create in me a pure heart, O God, and renew a steadfast spirit within me." This passage illustrates David's deep repentance and plea for renewal in the face of regret.

Moreover, the Bible provides a message of forgiveness and restoration, offering comfort to those weighed down by regret. 1 John 1:9 assures, "If we confess our sins, he is faithful and just and will forgive us our sins and purify us from all unrighteousness." This verse signifies the promise of God's forgiveness and cleansing for those who sincerely repent and seek reconciliation.

Furthermore, the Bible emphasizes the importance of learning from past mistakes and using regret as a catalyst for positive change. Philippians 3:13-14 encourages believers to press on, stating, "But one thing I do: Forgetting what is behind and straining toward what is ahead, I press on toward the goal to win the prize for which God has called me heavenward in Christ Jesus." This passage underscores the idea of moving forward, leaving behind regrets and focusing on growth and progress.

Additionally, the Bible offers narratives that demonstrate how individuals found redemption and a renewed sense of purpose despite past regrets. The story of Peter, who deeply regretted denying Jesus three times, showcases his eventual restoration and role as a prominent disciple. This narrative illustrates God's ability to turn regrets into opportunities for growth and service.

Ultimately, the Bible provides comfort to those experiencing regret by acknowledging the pain of past mistakes, offering the promise of forgiveness and renewal, encouraging individuals to learn from their regrets, and presenting stories of redemption and transformation. It instills hope by affirming that despite past regrets, God offers forgiveness, restoration, and a path forward toward a meaningful and purposeful life.

Then David said to God, 'I have sinned greatly by
doing this. Now, I beg you, take away the guilt of
your servant. I have done a very foolish thing.'
1 Chronicles 21:8

Repent, then, and turn to God, so that your sins may be wiped
out, that times of refreshing may come from the Lord.
Acts 3:19

I have declared to both Jews and Greeks that they must turn
to God in repentance and have faith in our Lord Jesus.
Acts 20:21

Therefore, you Israelites, I will judge each of you according
to your own ways, declares the Sovereign Lord. Repent! Turn
away from all your offenses; then sin will not be your downfall.
Ezekiel 18:30

This is what the Sovereign Lord, the Holy One of Israel,
says: 'In repentance and rest is your salvation, in quietness
and trust is your strength, but you would have none of it.'
Isaiah 30:15

Let the wicked forsake their ways and the unrighteous
their thoughts. Let them turn to the Lord, and he will have
mercy on them, and to our God, for he will freely pardon.
Isaiah 55:7

Come near to God, and he will come near to you. Wash
your hands, you sinners, and purify your hearts, you
double-minded. Grieve, mourn, and wail. Change your
laughter to mourning and your joy to gloom. Humble
yourselves before the Lord, and he will lift you up.
James 4:8-10

Again and again, I sent my servants the prophets, who
said, 'Do not do this detestable thing that I hate!'
Jeremiah 44:4

Therefore, I despise myself and repent in dust and ashes.
Job 42:6

Rend your heart and not your garments. Return to the Lord
your God, for he is gracious and compassionate, slow to anger
and abounding in love, and he relents from sending calamity.
Joel 2:13

For God so loved the world that he gave his one and only
Son, that whoever believes in him shall not perish but have
eternal life. For God did not send his Son into the world to
condemn the world, but to save the world through him.
John 3:16-17

But let people and animals be covered with sackcloth.
Let everyone call urgently on God. Let them give up their
evil ways and their violence. Who knows? God may yet
relent and with compassion turn from his fierce anger so
that we will not perish.' When God saw what they did and
how they turned from their evil ways, he relented and did
not bring on them the destruction he had threatened.
Jonah 3:8-10

In the same way, I tell you, there is rejoicing in the presence
of the angels of God over one sinner who repents.
Luke 15:10

But the tax collector stood at a distance. He would not
even look up to heaven, but beat his breast and said,
'God, have mercy on me, a sinner.' I tell you that this
man, rather than the other, went home justified before
God. For all those who exalt themselves will be humbled,
and those who humble themselves will be exalted.
Luke 18:13-14

And he went outside and wept bitterly.
Luke 22:62

Produce fruit in keeping with repentance.
Matthew 3:8

Then Peter remembered the word Jesus had spoken:
'Before the rooster crows, you will disown me three
times.' And he went outside and wept bitterly.
Matthew 26:75

Whoever conceals their sins does not prosper, but the
one who confesses and renounces them finds mercy.
Proverbs 28:13

Create in me a pure heart, O God, and
renew a steadfast spirit within me.
Psalm 51:10

My sacrifice, O God, is a broken spirit; a broken
and contrite heart you, God, will not despise.
Psalm 51:17

Consider how far you have fallen! Repent and do the
things you did at first. If you do not repent, I will come
to you and remove your lampstand from its place.
Revelation 2:5

Those whom I love I rebuke and discipline.
So be earnest and repent.
Revelation 3:19

Or do you show contempt for the riches of his kindness,
forbearance, and patience, not realizing that God's
kindness is intended to lead you to repentance?
Romans 2:4

What benefit did you reap at that time from the things
you are now ashamed of? Those things result in death!
Romans 6:21

Yet now I am happy, not because you were made sorry, but
because your sorrow led you to repentance. For you became
sorrowful as God intended and so were not harmed in any way
by us. Godly sorrow brings repentance that leads to salvation
and leaves no regret, but worldly sorrow brings death.
2 Corinthians 7:9-10

If my people, who are called by my name, will humble
themselves and pray and seek my face and turn from
their wicked ways, then I will hear from heaven, and
I will forgive their sin and will heal their land.
2 Chronicles 7:14

I am afraid that when I come again my God will humble
me before you, and I will be grieved over many who have
sinned earlier and have not repented of the impurity,
sexual sin, and debauchery in which they have indulged.
2 Corinthians 12:21

Peter replied, 'Repent and be baptized, every one of you,
in the name of Jesus Christ for the forgiveness of your
sins. And you will receive the gift of the Holy Spirit.'
Acts 2:38

Repent of this wickedness and pray to the Lord in the hope that
he may forgive you for having such a thought in your heart.
Acts 8:22

We have sinned and done wrong. We have
been wicked and have rebelled; we have turned
away from your commands and laws.
Daniel 9:5

Sorrow is better than laughter, because
a sad face is good for the heart.
Ecclesiastes 7:3

And do not grieve the Holy Spirit of God, with whom
you were sealed for the day of redemption.
Ephesians 4:30

The Lord regretted that he had made human beings
on the earth, and his heart was deeply troubled.
Genesis 6:6

Come, let us return to the Lord. He has torn us to pieces but he
will heal us; he has injured us but he will bind up our wounds.
Hosea 6:1

Therefore confess your sins to each other and pray
for each other so that you may be healed. The prayer
of a righteous person is powerful and effective.
James 5:16

But if I say, 'I will not mention his word or speak anymore
in his name,' his word is in my heart like a fire, a fire shut up
in my bones. I am weary of holding it in; indeed, I cannot.
Jeremiah 20:9

I have listened attentively, but they do not say what
is right. None of them repent of their wickedness,
saying, 'What have I done?' Each pursues their
own course like a horse charging into battle.
Jeremiah 8:6

After I strayed, I repented; after I came to understand,
I beat my breast. I was ashamed and humiliated
because I bore the disgrace of my youth.
Jeremiah 31:19

"Even now," declares the Lord, "return to me with all your
heart, with fasting and weeping and mourning." Rend your
heart and not your garments. Return to the Lord your God,
for he is gracious and compassionate, slow to anger and
abounding in love, and he relents from sending calamity.
Joel 2:12-13

I tell you, no! But unless you repent, you too will all perish.
Luke 13:3

When he came to his senses, he said, 'How
many of my father's hired servants have food to
spare, and here I am starving to death!'
Luke 15:17

"The time has come," he said. "The kingdom of God
has come near. Repent and believe the good news!"
Mark 1:15

When Judas, who had betrayed him, saw that Jesus was
condemned, he was seized with remorse and returned the
thirty pieces of silver to the chief priests and the elders.
'I have sinned,' he said, 'for I have betrayed innocent
blood.' 'What is that to us?' they replied. 'That's your
responsibility.' So Judas threw the money into the temple
and left. Then he went away and hanged himself.
Matthew 27:3-5

These passages illustrate instances of remorse, repentance, and
the call to turn away from wrongdoing, seek forgiveness, and return
to God. They express the feelings of regret and the opportunity for
redemption and reconciliation through repentance and turning
toward God's mercy and grace.

PART TEN: SHAME

ABOUT SHAME

Shame, a powerful and distressing emotion often associated with feelings of disgrace, humiliation, or guilt, can deeply impact an individual's sense of self-worth and identity. The Bible addresses the experience of shame and offers solace, forgiveness, and restoration to those burdened by its weight.

The Bible acknowledges the reality of shame and the human tendency to feel unworthy or condemned due to past mistakes or wrongdoing. However, it also presents a message of redemption and forgiveness. Romans 10:11 assures, "Anyone who believes in him will never be put to shame." This verse highlights the transformative power of faith, suggesting that belief in God brings freedom from the shame that arises from one's past.

Moreover, the Bible emphasizes the concept of repentance and the opportunity for renewal through God's grace. In Isaiah 54:4, it states, "Do not be afraid; you will not be put to shame. Do not fear disgrace; you will not be humiliated. You will forget the shame of your youth and remember no more the reproach of your widowhood." This verse offers hope by promising a release from past shame and a new beginning through God's mercy.

Additionally, the Bible showcases stories of individuals who experienced shame but found forgiveness and restoration through God's grace. One such story is that of the prodigal son in Luke 15:20-24, where despite his mistakes and shame, he is welcomed back with love and celebration by his father. This narrative illustrates God's unconditional love and willingness to restore those burdened by shame.

Furthermore, the Bible highlights the importance of seeking refuge and strength in God amidst feelings of shame. Psalm 34:5 affirms, "Those who look to him are radiant; their faces are never covered with shame." This verse encourages individuals to turn to God for comfort and assurance, believing that He can transform their shame into a sense of radiance and dignity.

Ultimately, the Bible provides comfort to those experiencing shame by offering the promise of forgiveness, redemption, and a fresh start through faith in God. It emphasizes the transformative power of God's grace and love, providing hope for those burdened by the weight of shame, assuring them that through Him, there is healing and restoration from feelings of disgrace or unworthiness.

Do not be afraid; you will not be put to shame. Do
not fear disgrace; you will not be humiliated. You
will forget the shame of your youth and remember
no more the reproach of your widowhood.
Isaiah 54:4

As Scripture says, 'Anyone who believes in
him will never be put to shame.'
Romans 10:11

Those who look to him are radiant; their
faces are never covered with shame.
Psalm 34:5

Instead of your shame, you will receive a double
portion, and instead of disgrace, you will rejoice in your
inheritance. And so, you will inherit a double portion
in your land, and everlasting joy will be yours.
Isaiah 61:7

The wise inherit honor, but fools get only shame.
Proverbs 3:35

Let us lie down in our shame, and let our disgrace
cover us. We have sinned against the Lord our God,
both we and our ancestors; from our youth till this
day we have not obeyed the Lord our God.
Jeremiah 3:25

You will have plenty to eat until you are full, and you will praise
the name of the Lord your God, who has worked wonders for
you; never again will my people be shamed. Then you will
know that I am in Israel, that I am the Lord your God, and
that there is no other; never again will my people be shamed.
Joel 2:26-27

For I am not ashamed of the gospel, because it is the
power of God that brings salvation to everyone who
believes: first to the Jew, then to the Gentile.
Romans 1:16

Then I would not be put to shame when
I consider all your commands.
Psalm 119:6

I eagerly expect and hope that I will in no way be ashamed,
but will have sufficient courage so that now as always Christ
will be exalted in my body, whether by life or by death.
Philippians 1:20

However, if you suffer as a Christian, do not be
ashamed, but praise God that you bear that name.
1 Peter 4:16

So do not be ashamed of the testimony about our
Lord or of me his prisoner. Rather, join with me in
suffering for the gospel, by the power of God.
2 Timothy 1:8

But you give us victory over our enemies;
you put our adversaries to shame.
Psalm 44:7

As it is written: 'See, I lay in Zion a stone that causes
people to stumble and a rock that makes them fall, and
the one who believes in him will never be put to shame.'
Romans 9:33

Multitudes who sleep in the dust of the earth will awake: some
to everlasting life, others to shame and everlasting contempt.
Daniel 12:2

And now, dear children, continue in him, so
that when he appears we may be confident and
unashamed before him at his coming.
1 John 2:28

Therefore, this is what the Lord, who redeemed Abraham,
says to the descendants of Jacob: 'No longer will Jacob
be ashamed; no longer will their faces grow pale.'
Isaiah 29:22

If anyone is ashamed of me and my words in this adulterous
and sinful generation, the Son of Man will be ashamed of them
when he comes in his Father's glory with the holy angels.
Mark 8:38

You who boast in the law, do you dishonor God by
breaking the law? As it is written: 'God's name is
blasphemed among the Gentiles because of you.'
Romans 2:23-24

For even if I boast somewhat freely about the authority
the Lord gave us for building you up rather than
tearing you down, I will not be ashamed of it.
2 Corinthians 10:8

It is shameful even to mention what
the disobedient do in secret.
Ephesians 5:12

You will be filled with shame instead of glory. Now
it is your turn! Drink and let your nakedness be
exposed! The cup from the Lord's right hand is coming
around to you, and disgrace will cover your glory.
Habakkuk 2:16

All who rage against you will surely be ashamed and disgraced;
those who oppose you will be as nothing and perish.
Isaiah 41:11

For in Scripture, it says: 'See, I lay a stone in Zion,
a chosen and precious cornerstone, and the one
who trusts in him will never be put to shame.'
1 Peter 2:6

The wise will be put to shame; they will be dismayed
and trapped. Since they have rejected the word of
the Lord, what kind of wisdom do they have?
Jeremiah 8:9

When David was told about this, he sent messengers to meet
the men, for they were greatly humiliated. The king said, 'Stay
at Jericho till your beards have grown, and then come back.'
2 Samuel 10:5

All the makers of idols will be put to shame and
disgraced; they will go off into disgrace together.
Isaiah 45:16

The righteous hate what is false, but the wicked make
themselves a stench and bring shame on themselves.
Proverbs 13:5

We are disgraced, for we have been insulted and
shame covers our faces because foreigners have
entered the holy places of the Lord's house.
Jeremiah 51:51

May those who hope in you not be disgraced because of
me, Lord, the Lord Almighty; may those who seek you
not be put to shame because of me, God of Israel.
Psalm 69:6

Saul's anger flared up at Jonathan, and he said to him,
'You son of a perverse and rebellious woman! Don't I know
that you have sided with the son of Jesse to your own
shame and to the shame of the mother who bore you?'
1 Samuel 20:30

Lord, you are righteous, but this day, we are covered with
shame—the people of Judah and the inhabitants of Jerusalem
and all Israel, both near and far, in all the countries where
you have scattered us because of our unfaithfulness to you.
Daniel 9:7

Then, when I make atonement for you for all you
have done, you will remember and be ashamed
and never again open your mouth because of your
humiliation, declares the Sovereign Lord.
Ezekiel 16:63

I want you to know that I am not doing this for your
sake, declares the Sovereign Lord. Be ashamed and
disgraced for your conduct, people of Israel!
Ezekiel 36:32

But now that you have been set free from sin and
have become slaves of God, the benefit you reap
leads to holiness, and the result is eternal life.
Romans 6:22

Lord, you are the hope of Israel; all who forsake you
will be put to shame. Those who turn away from
you will be written in the dust because they have
forsaken the Lord, the spring of living water.
Jeremiah 17:13

Then my enemy will see it and will be covered with
shame, she who said to me, 'Where is the Lord your
God?' My eyes will see her downfall; even now she will
be trampled underfoot like mire in the streets.
Micah 7:10

Are they ashamed of their detestable conduct? No, they
have no shame at all; they do not even know how to
blush. So, they will fall among the fallen; they will be
brought down when I punish them,' says the Lord.
Jeremiah 6:15

I myself will lift up your skirts over your
face that your shame may be seen.
Jeremiah 13:26

They are distressed because they had been confident;
they arrive there, only to be disappointed.
Job 6:20

Son of man, describe the temple to the people
of Israel, that they may be ashamed of their
sins. Let them consider its perfection.
Ezekiel 43:10

"I am against you," declares the Lord Almighty. "I will
lift your skirts over your face. I will show the nations
your nakedness and the kingdoms your shame."
Nahum 3:5

But the Lord is with me like a mighty warrior; so, my
persecutors will stumble and not prevail. They will fail and be
thoroughly disgraced; their dishonor will never be forgotten.
Jeremiah 20:11

The wind will drive all your shepherds away, and your
allies will go into exile. Then you will be ashamed
and disgraced because of all your wickedness.
Jeremiah 22:22

It will be carried to Assyria as tribute for the
great king. Ephraim will be disgraced; Israel
will be ashamed of its foreign alliances.
Hosea 10:6

Nations will see and be ashamed, deprived of all
their power. They will put their hands over their
mouths and their ears will become deaf.
Micah 7:16

These passages highlight various contexts in which shame is
discussed in the Bible, addressing both the experience of shame and
the hope of redemption and deliverance from shame through God's
grace and mercy.

R

Thank you for purchasing ***Bible Of Comfort: Biblical Wisdom for Healing During Troubled Times*** by University Scholastic Press. We sincerely hope you found some relief from your troubles.

If you enjoyed this book, please consider spreading your good word so we can help others on their healing journey.

Check out some of our other coloring books, journals, planners and cookbooks brought to you by University Scholastic Press, an international printer and press, world-renowned for its myriad of original creative non-fiction books, study guides, workbooks, cookbooks, journals and planners.

Thank you again for your purchase.

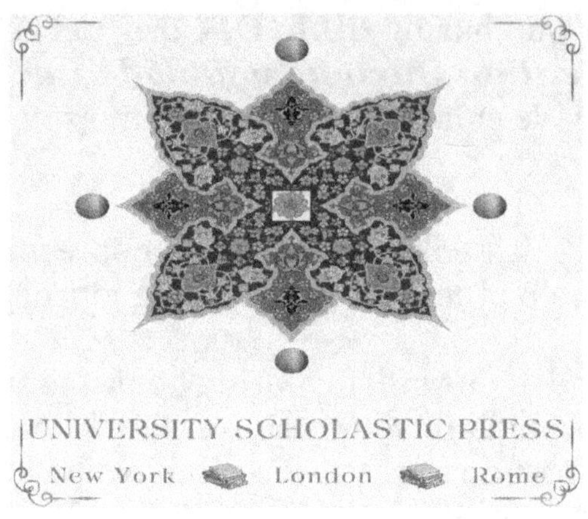

Copyright 2024 University Scholastic Press